Cryptocurrency

A Straightforward Tutorial That Will Teach You How To
Make Your Very First Investment In Bitcoin Or Ethereum
Today

*(Managing Your Way Through The Convergence Of
Gaming And Cryptocurrency)*

KlemensHinteregger

TABLE OF CONTENT

How The Use Of Technical Analysis Can Be Beneficial To Traders

A great number of investors have found that technical analysis is a helpful tool for risk management, which may be a significant barrier. Once a trader has an understanding of the concepts and principles of technical analysis, it is possible for this method to be used to any market, which makes it a flexible logical tool. Technical analysis seeks to discover patterns, while fundamental analysis attempts to find distinctive value in a market. Patterns, which may be usefully brought about by basics, are the focus of technical analysis.

The following are some of the benefits that come with making use of technical analysis:

Can be used to analyse any market over any time period.

The method of independent technique is available via the application of technical analysis.

Traders are able to differentiate trends while keeping an eye out for them.

In the context of Technical Analysis, Utilising Charts

A candle chart for the EUR/USD currency pair is shown below. This chart can be seen further down the page.

The development of technical analysis allowed for the prediction of future price trends across a variety of business sectors. In today's rapidly changing markets, it serves as the cornerstone of analysis for a number of different types of traders.

Technical analysis and fundamental analysis are two types of study that traders and other financial people use to try to anticipate future price movements. In this article, we will look at the first of the two that are available. In this tutorial, which will be significantly enlarged from its previous iteration, we will talk about a broad variety of technical analysis indicators.

When it's all said and done, a significant number of traders combine the methodologies of fundamental and technical research. Despite this, there are others who believe that one method is superior to the other and more effective. In any event, and regardless of whether you are a fundamentalist to the core, you can't ignore the fact that countless traders use technical analysis and follow through on respect for certain critical price levels. This is the case even if you are a fundamentalist to the core. In addition, this has the potential to influence the market in the opposite direction suggested by primary research alone. If a sufficient number of people believe that a certain technological aspect deserves to be relevant, then it will surely

Getting Your Footing In The World Of Cryptocurrency

It's possible that you have some extra cash that you may put towards investing in cryptocurrencies, but the question is: how will you do it? Exchanges, often known as digital currency exchanges (DCE), are the gateways via which crypto-worlds may be accessed by users. You have access to a diverse range of trading venues because to the abundance of exchanges now available on the market. However, before you make the decision to get one, there are a few things you should be aware of first.

Status or renown

You should begin by learning as much as possible about the DCE's background and history. What do individuals have to say about the services that they provide? Has there ever been an attempt to hack the exchange? How reliable and safe are the services that they provide? Reddit and Twitter are both fantastic resources of information, and you should consult them if you are interested in determining the credibility of different cryptocurrency exchanges.

Possibility of Access

The availability of the exchange in your region is yet another factor that you must take into consideration. Because certain exchanges do not work with customers from other countries, it is important to research which ones are available to you depending on where you are located.

The Rates of Exchange

Exchange rates might differ from one digital currency marketplace to the next. Researching at least three to four different DCEs is a good idea if you want to receive the best deal.

Protection and Assurance

You should use a trading platform that verifies your identification if you are worried about the stability and protection of your money. Traders on these platforms are often required to provide identification for verification purposes. Exchanges of anonymous digital money are far less safe and secure compared to this method, even if it may take some time. Always bear in mind that the money you are investing was earned through your own efforts. It is common sense to go the additional mile to ensure everyone's well-being.

As an example, let's look at Coinbase, which is now the most widely used bitcoin exchange. Using this platform to begin trading may be accomplished in the following manner:

Signing Up For It

Creating an account with Coinbase is a straightforward procedure. Simply clicking the "Sign Up" button that is located on the home page of the website is all that is required to get started. Almost immediately after that, the website will take you to a screen where you will be required to provide the following information:

Initials and Surname of Person

Email Username and Password

Mark the box to attest that you are at least 18 years old and that you agree to their assortment of terms and conditions.

The Process of Verification

A verification link will be sent to the email address you provided by the site. Simply clicking on it will take you to a website where you can verify your account information. After entering your cellphone number, you will be prompted to wait for a verification code. Simply enter the code that was supplied to you by SMS, and you will be all set.

Introducing a New Payment Option

Coinbase gives you a number of different payment alternatives to choose from, such as wire transfers, bank account debit cards, and debit cards.

Checking of Identification

Before you are allowed to make any purchases with your debit card, the exchange platform requires its members to provide evidence of their identities. You are required to comply with KYC and AML requirements in order to use Coinbase since it is a regulated corporation. There is no need for concern on your part since the procedure is really easy to understand.

Coinbase is one of the most user-friendly and accessible wallets available. After you have completed the steps, you will instantly be able to trade and exchange a variety of cryptocurrencies, including Bitcoin, Ethereum, Bitcoin Cash, and Litecoin.

Public Addresses As Well As Private Keys

When we wish to move money from one person to another in a digital monetary system, the first thing we have to figure out is how to set up accounts for both parties.

HOW DOES THE DELEGATED ACCOUNT MANAGEMENT PROCESS ACTUALLY WORK?

You are provided with a bank account number in order for other individuals to give you money via the banking system. Nobody else has the same bank account number as you do; in fact, no two people can have the same number. If you did not change this setting, the person to whom you submitted your account number in order for them to send you money would get the money instead of you. The same is true for electronic mail: When you sign up for a service, like Gmail for instance, the service will check to see whether the email address you provide has already been taken. This is done to prevent address conflicts. This is only possible because of the centralised nature of services such as banks and email providers like Gmail. As long as they do their duties responsibly, everything will be OK. But what happens if the bank chooses to just terminate your account, or if Gmail stops allowing you to view your emails? What if the centralised service decides to abuse the authority it has been given?

Because there is no centralised authority that controls access to the account database, this particular scenario simply cannot take place in a decentralised system. It is not possible for it to exclude you or take something away from you. But how exactly does it prevent it from happening that two individuals in such a system would wind up with the same "address"? The majority of people are unaware of a few of genuine innovations that have been made in the realm of blockchain technology. When I think about it, this address solution is one of the things that gives me genuine excitement over and over again.

The use of cryptography in conjunction with a private key and a public address provides the solution.

The Time Required for Trading Varies.

Day trading often requires a lot more time than other forms of trading do, despite the fact that both types of trading need an expenditure of some amount of time. Day traders often engage in trading for a minimum of two hours during the course of each trading day. If you include in time for planning as well as chart and trade analysis, you should prepare to spend at least three to four hours in front of the computer. If a day trader decides to engage in the activity for more than a few hours each day, the time commitment required to do so balloons dramatically, and the activity morphs into a full-day job.

Swing trading, on the other hand, may be completed in a much shorter amount of time. For example, if you are swing trading off of a daily chart, you may find fresh trades and alter orders based on current events in around forty-five minutes each night. It's possible that you won't have to do these workouts on a daily basis.

Some traders who engage in swing trading, in which they take trades that last weeks or months, may only need to search for trades and update orders once every week. This reduces the time commitment to approximately an hour out of each week rather than every night, and it also means that refreshing orders may not be required on a daily basis.

Day trading is a kind of trading that you should engage in when the market is open and active. Specific periods of the day are considered to be optimal for day trading. These times are restricted. Choose swing trading as a more advantageous option to day trading in the event that you are unable to trade during those specific hours. Swing traders have the ability to look for trades or spot orders at any time of the day, often far after the market has closed for the day.

Swing traders are less susceptible to the impact of constant second-to-second fluctuations in the pricing of an edge. They focus on the overall strategy and often look at day-by-day charts; hence, placing trades after the market ends on a particular day does quite well for them. Day traders earn money off of changes that occur second by second; thus, they need to be included when the action is taking place.

The Hodl Strategy Taken In A Passive Manner

As soon as you have the means to HODL, you will essentially be ready to wait until the time when one bitcoin is equivalent to one million dollars in US currency. You may simply sell your funds there and there, and utilise the money from the sale to purchase a property with the profit. The only need at this point is obviously for Bitcoin's value to increase to this point. This is something that might take place, but it's not certain to. Nobody can predict the future with absolute precision, but if you choose to invest in HOLD, your goal should be to gamble that it will continue to increase in value over time (regardless of how much its price shifts).

The passive HODL strategy is keeping your money put away and waiting for anything like this to take place. after it comes to this particular investment, the task at hand is finished after you have purchased your cryptocurrency using traditional currency and then moved it to a digital wallet that is (at least somewhat) safe. After this has occurred, all that is left for you to do is determine what would constitute a winning point for you or at what price you would cash out. If you are currently holding, for instance, 0.1 BTC that you purchased for $1000, then $1 million seems like a solid position to be in to accomplish that. But what if the price keeps to up even after it reaches one million US dollars? Perhaps the price of Bitcoin will reach $1.1 in one week's time, and $1.5 in one month's time after that. Or, maybe it will fall below nine hundred thousand dollars and won't start to rise back up for many months, if it ever returns at all.

Every passive HODL strategy need to include an exit point, which is a time at which the investor not only recoups their initial investment but also makes a profit. Keep in mind that any profit you make will only be legitimate after you have actually sold your crypto assets and obtained the resulting fiat dollars. The disparity between this and the potential profit is striking. It's possible that you're sitting on some bitcoin that you acquired for X dollars but can now sell for 10 times that amount in your digital wallet. But so long as the cryptocurrency funds are not transferred to an exchange where they can be exchanged, this kind of profit can only be described as being hypothetical. The issue is that the mindset of tracking the daily market swings to determine how successful (or unsuccessful) your investment selection was may ultimately push you towards being a trader, which is something you want to avoid doing as much as possible. That is why every investor, even the hardcore HODL club members have to have a defined exit strategy and a predefined price when they would sell their assets. This is the point at which they go from having a potential profit to having a profit in the real world.

A reasonable goal would be anything that is greater than the amount of money that you initially invested (less any fees associated with the trade or transaction). As long as you take out more fiat money that you put in, you're winning at the HODL game, and do not let anyone tell you otherwise. Imagine for a moment that you cashed out at $1 million, only to go back a year later and learn that BTC had reached $3 million. You do not need to have a lot of imagination to picture oneself genuinely lamenting the fact that you did not remain around for a while longer and get three times the benefit that you earned in this manner. Because of this, an improved version of the HODL investing procedure has been developed.

The Most Widely Used Cryptosystem

The following two categories may be used to classify the many cryptocurrencies currently in circulation: Coins are produced on its blockchain and are intended to function as a kind of money in the future. As an example, Ether is a kind of cryptocurrency that was developed on the Ethereum network.

The term "Altcoin" refers to any cryptocurrency that is not Bitcoin and is based on the blockchain. To abbreviate the phrase "alternative to Bitcoin," the term "altcoin" was created. Most alternative cryptocurrencies were developed as an attempt to enhance Bitcoin in some way. Examples of alternative cryptocurrencies include: Namecoin, Peercoin, Litecoin (LTC), Ethereum, and USD Coin (USDC).

Some cryptocurrencies, such as Bitcoin, have a fixed supply of coins, which helps to foster an ongoing demand for them and adds credence to their perceived value. For instance, the ultimate amount of Bitcoin that may be mined has been set at 21 million, as specified by whomever or whatever invented Bitcoin.

Tokens are programmable assets that allow the formulation and execution of one-of-a-kind intelligent contracts. Tokens are created on a blockchain that was just recently developed. Contracts, which exist on the blockchain's periphery and may be used to verify ownership of assets, can be employed in this context. Tokens may both be transferred and received, and they can be used to represent a variety of different units of value, including money, coins, digital assets, and power.

Stablecoins are digital currencies whose values are pegged to those of other currencies or assets, such as gold. Stablecoins provide users with a mechanism to sell their cryptocurrency into a help bearing the same value as a national currency, but which can still be transacted and held in a manner similar to that of cryptocurrency inside the ecosystem. Most often, stablecoins are linked one-to-one with the United States dollar.

Another sort of cryptocurrency, referred to as nonfungible tokens (NFTs), are distinguished by the fact that each token is unique and cannot be exchanged for anything else. For example, a Bitcoin is fungible, which means that it may be exchanged for another Bitcoin and you would still get the same exact product. On the other side, a one-of-a-kind trading card can never be reproduced in any other way. If you exchanged it for a different card, you would get something completely different in return.

Depending on the outcomes you want to achieve, it can be necessary to investigate the nature and purpose of a particular asset before dealing with it. Not all digital assets were developed with the intention of being invested in.

In the present day, many users of cryptocurrency understand and appreciate these nuances, but traders and lay investors may not recognise the difference, since all forms of token tend to trade in the same manner on cryptocurrency exchanges, Bitcoins being the exception.

Bitcoin is a completely digital form of money that is also often referred to as a cryptocurrency, a virtual currency, or a digital currency. All of these terms refer to the same thing.

It may be thought of as the digital equivalent of currency. You are able to spend it on a variety of goods and services; but, very few retailers now accept Bitcoin, and many nations have outright banned the cryptocurrency.

On the other hand, there are businesses that are beginning to acknowledge its expanding influence.

For example, in October of the previous year, the online payment firm PayPal announced that it will soon enable its clients to purchase and trade bitcoins.

Bitcoin Cash (BCH)

Ethereum, the first alternative to Bitcoin on our list, is a decentralised software platform that enables the creation and operation of smart contracts and decentralised applications (dapps) without the possibility of downtime, fraud, control, or intervention from a third party. The goal of Ethereum is to create a decentralised suite of financial goods that anybody in the world, regardless of their country, ethnicity, or religion, may gladly access. This is the vision that drives Ethereum's development.2 The fact that individuals in some countries who lack access to state infrastructure and state designations may get access to bank accounts, loans, insurance, or any combination of other financial goods makes the necessity of this feature all the more appealing.

The apps that run on Ethereum make use of Ether, the cryptographic token that is unique to the Ethereum platform. Ether is analogous to a vehicle for getting about on the Ethereum platform. It is primarily geared at developers who want to construct and operate apps within Ethereum, or, more recently, at investors who are wanting to make purchases of other digital currencies using Ether. Ether is now the second-largest digital currency by market capitalization after Bitcoin, but it trails behind the dominating cryptocurrency by a wide margin. Ether was introduced in 2015, and it is currently the second-largest digital currency after Bitcoin.3 As of November 2021, the demand limit for Ether is less than half that of Bitcoin's, despite the fact that Ether is trading at over $4,000 per ETH.4

In 2014, Ethereum launched a presale for Ether, which was met with a very positive response. This event was significant in the birth of the initial coin offering (ICO) age. The Ethereum website claims that it can be used to "codify, decentralise, protected, and trade just about anything."5 After the hacking attack on the decentralised autonomous community (DAO) in 2016, Ethereum was forked into two distinct cryptocurrencies: Ethereum (ETH) and Ethereum Classic (ETC).

In 2021, Ethereum changed its agreement method from proof-of-work (PoW) to proof-of-stake (PoS). PoW stood for proof of work, while PoS stood for proof of stake.6 It is intended that this change would enable Ethereum's network to operate itself using a great deal less energy, enhance the speed at which transactions take place, and create an economic climate that is more conducive to deflation. The Proof-of-Stake protocol makes it possible for network participants to "stake" their Ether on the network. Those who are successful in doing so will get Ether, which functions very similarly to a thrilling account. This strategy contributes to the maintenance of the network and the processing of the transactions that take place. This is an alternative to the proof-of-work technique that is used by Bitcoin, in which miners are paid with more Bitcoin for the processing of transactions.

**Designed To Keep The Government In
Perpetual Financial Servitude.**

The only way the economy of the United
States can get into debt is if it chooses to do
so. People frequently predict that the
government would just create an unlimited
amount of money in order to pay off all of
the government's obligations. This is a
common belief among most people.
However, the Fed's system would not let
anything like this to occur. The Federal
Reserve is the entity that is responsible for
the issuance of new money; not the United
States government.

Because of this, they are known as notes
issued by the Federal Reserve. When the
government needs more money, it will
simply have to take on more debt. There is
no other way to generate more money.

To a greater extent than the public interest, favours private interests.

It is often held that private interests and lobby organisations tend to have a considerable degree of influence over the Federal Reserve, and this belief is supported by some evidence. Because of this, only certain people would stand to gain, rather than the society as a whole. The Federal Reserve is a government organisation, but it is nevertheless managed by people who have a focus on business, and this leaves the door open for corruption to find its way into the organisation.

It is not widely agreed upon that something is useful or valid.

discussions have taken place all around the globe over whether or not it is constitutional to have a national bank. These discussions have taken place to the degree that the federal government is able to manage and plan the economy by using the national bank.

There has been a great deal of criticism levelled at the Central Bank throughout its existence, directed mostly at the policies that it has developed and put into effect. Some individuals are even under the impression that the country's high unemployment rate is directly attributable to the nation's excessively stringent monetary policy.

Stability will be increased as a result.

The Federal Reserve has, against popular assumption to the contrary, been successful in calming bank panics. However, a significant number of individuals hold the view that the country's central bank is unable to successfully handle the nation's monetary policy, and that this contributes to an increased level of instability.

Others say that it interferes too much in the economy, while others believe that it is very accommodating to the political administration. Some believe that it is highly accommodating to the political administration.

Manipulates the economy of the United States

Because of its ability to raise or lower interest rates, it may either hasten or slow down economic expansion depending on how it is used.

Additionally, it has the potential to inflate the economy before causing it to burst. The majority of American residents have a tendency to place responsibility for the state of the economy on the president, despite the fact that these leaders do not actually have that much power over the economy in comparison to the Federal Reserve.

The aforementioned benefits and drawbacks of the Federal Reserve System in the United States need to be weighed against one another in order to arrive at an informed conclusion on whether or not the Federal Reserve System is useful.

Risk for Insurance

There is not a single federal or government-run programme that guarantees bitcoin exchanges or accounts. According to SFOX, it will begin providing investors in bitcoin with FDIC protection in 2019. On the other hand, it would only be applied to the parts of the transactions that included cash. SFOX is both a premier dealer of cryptocurrencies and one of the most prominent trading platforms in the industry.

Threat of Fraud

Despite the fact that the authentication of owners and the registration of transactions are both accomplished via the use of the private key encryption, there have been instances documented in which con artists sold customers phoney bitcoins. For instance, in July of 2013, the SEC initiated legal proceedings in response to a Ponzi scam using bitcoin. In addition to that, there have been instances of the price of bitcoinbeing artificially manipulated. The manipulation of the price of bitcoin is another typical sort of fraud.

Risk to the Market

As with any other kind of investment, the value of bitcoins is subject to significant fluctuations. Bitcoin's value has been subject to a great deal of volatility throughout its brief history. Because of its primary emphasis on achieving the highest possible volume of trading on exchanges, it has a high degree of sensitivity to any happening that warrants coverage in the news. According to the Consumer Financial Protection Bureau, the price of bitcoin dropped by 61% in only one day in 2013. In 2014, the percentage that a price dropped in only one day was around 80%.

If the majority of people continue to ignore bitcoin as a kind of cash, the value of this digital currency is going to plummet, and it will eventually become worthless. When the price of bitcoin dropped from its all-time high amid the growth in the value of cryptocurrencies in late 2017 and early 2018, there was widespread speculation that the "bitcoin bubble" had finally burst.

When you take into account how much competition there is in the market, you will see that there is a lot of it. Bitcoin is now in the lead among cryptocurrencies, however there are many more to choose from. This is because to the popularity of its brand and the money it has raised from venture capitalists; nonetheless, there is always a risk that a technical advance would introduce a superior virtual currency.

On April 14, 2021, the price of a bitcoin hit an all-time high of $64,863.

Fragmentation among the Community of Cryptocurrency

Since the inception of bitcoin, there have been a number of occasions in which disagreements between camps of miners and developers have triggered divisions across the board in the community of cryptocurrencies. The vast majority of incidents involving these communities of Bitcoin users and miners have resulted in a modification to the protocol underlying the Bitcoin network.

A technique known as "forking" is used to generate any new kind of bitcoin that also receives a new moniker for itself. This division has the potential to be a "hard fork." In the case of a hard fork, a new cryptocurrency retains the same transaction history as bitcoin up to a certain moment in time, after which a new token is generated. Bitcoin Cash, which was created in August of 2017, Bitcoin Gold, which was created in October of 2017, and Bitcoin SV, which was created in November of 2017, are all examples of cryptocurrencies that were created as a result of a cryptocurrency's hard fork.

The modification of the protocol known as a "soft fork" ensures that it will continue to function according to the same guidelines as the previous version of the system. Soft forks of bitcoin, for instance, have introduced new features, such as the segregated witness (SegWit) protocol.

Why is a Bitcoin Investment Worth It?

Bitcoin does have a significant value. Within a little more than a decade, its price went from $1 to more than $50,000, indicating a tremendous surge in demand. Bitcoin's high value may be attributed to a variety of factors, the most important of which are its limited supply, the tremendous demand for it on the market, and the very low cost of producing bitcoins. Although they cannot be physically touched, bitcoins have a market valuation of one trillion dollars as of 2021.

Is Buying Bitcoin a Fraud?

Bitcoins are a genuine kind of currency. Even if you can't physically interact with them since they are virtual, you should nonetheless consider them to be real. Since the first bitcoin was mined, there have been 10 years since that event. The source code that is utilised to operate the system is available for download and is open-source. Anyone is free to examine the code for errors or other indications of unethical behaviour. There is a possibility that some errors may occur, but these errors will not be caused by bitcoins themselves; rather, they will be caused by human error or by any third-party programme that is being used.

What Is the Current Supply of Bitcoins?

By the year 2140, the total number of Bitcoins that will have been mined will amount to 21 million. At this time, there have been more over 18.8 million bitcoins mined, which accounts for about 90 percentof the total. According to the findings of certain researchers, around 20 percent of the bitcoins that have been mined have vanished. That is something that may occur for a variety of different causes. Those bitcoins might have been lost for a number of reasons, including the passing away of the owner, the forgetting of the owner's private key, or the transfer of bitcoins to addresses that are no longer in use.

Should the 'B' in Bitcoin Be Capitalised?

It is customary to refer to a Bitcoin network, system, or protocol with a capital "B" when doing so. By convention, you must always use a tiny "b" if you are referring to individual bitcoins or to bitcoins as a unit.

Where Can I Make a Bitcoin Purchase?

Bitcoins may be acquired via the use of internet exchanges. ATMs that accept Bitcoin transactions are increasingly becoming commonplace all over the globe. You may buy bitcoins with cash or a credit card at kiosks that are linked to the internet and can be found in many public places. You could also be able to buy bitcoins from a friend or acquaintance of yours.

Mining Syndicates

Because mining demands a significant amount of processing power, miners will often work together in groups in order to pool their resources and achieve more successful outcomes. If the pool is successful in removing a block, the reward should be distributed among its participants, often in proportion to the amount of computing power and effort that each participant contributed to the operation. Due to the ever-increasing complexity of the process, the most frequent method for mining Bitcoin at the moment is participating in a mining pool.

The behaviour of mining pools might vary greatly from one another. It is possible to circumvent efforts at centralization via the use of peer-to-peer mining pools. The pool creates a second blockchain on which data relating to the mining is posted; this allows the data to be referred to inside the pool, which helps to ensure that the majority vote is kept.

The most popular kind of mining pool is the proportional mining pool, which was also the one we used as an example in the previous section. The gathering of computers takes place apart from the peer-to-peer interaction, and miners only get their rewards when the block has been successfully mined.

The Pay-Per-Share mining pool is the third and final kind of mining pool. It is similar to proportional mining pools, with the key difference being that miners get compensated regardless of whether or not the block is successfully mined. This is the method of pooling resources that is the most centralised.

The majority of mining pools designate a mining operator who is responsible for delegating work. At this point, it is essential to bear in mind a variety of factors, including the pool's resources, the capabilities of its systems, and the number of individuals that are participating in it. An operator is expected to be forthright about fees and other measurables, such as the success rate and the level of complexity of the hash.

For instance, larger pool sizes could make it simpler to extract blocks than smaller pool sizes, but participants still need to be on board with the way that incentives are doled out. When there are more individuals, there are fewer heavier duties, which leads to proportionately fewer obligations and lesser rewards. If a person's primary concern is mining and they measure their success by the quantity of cryptocurrency they are able to extract, then a huge pool is likely to be the most suitable option for them. A slower payout rate but greater total payouts for all participants might be expected from pools of a smaller size. The BTC network functions best with smaller pools since they are simpler and easier to operate in a decentralised manner. Be wary of "bandwidth clogging" inside the blockchain network if you choose for a bigger pool size. This may occur when there are more transactions than the network can handle. This occurs when there is an excessive concentration of computing resources inside a single section of a network. It is not a desirable situation to have, which is why careful consideration need to be given to the dimensions of the swimming pool.

Other aspects that need to be taken into account include how well secured the pool is from assaults and how resilient it would be if it were to come under attack by a hacker. It is not unusual for hacker organisations to target mining pools; thus, you should take into mind the dangers and find out how the operator of your mining pool responds to assaults of this sort.

Mining will only get more difficult since there is a decreasing quantity of BTC, which is why mining pools are a significant alternative for the future. They imply a lower individual investment in technology in exchange for an increase in the number of opportunities to extract blocks and be paid for doing so. It is essential to keep in mind that joining a mining pool will result in the loss of some of your autonomy and will need you to play by the rules established by the pool's strongest members. This will often result in a lower payout when compared to the other members of the pool.

Swap conventional money for an alternative cryptocurrency.

You will need cryptocurrency if you want to be able to participate in initial coin offerings (ICOs). Ethereum and Bitcoin are now the most widely used ones. Take into consideration the fact that the start-up converts the money invested into fiat currency in order to pay for things like expenses and advancements, among other things.

Investing in an ICO

Keep in mind that many firms do not accept Ether or Bitcoin when they ask you to send cryptocurrencies to a particular address. This is something you should keep in mind if the company asks you to transfer cryptocurrencies. There are certain exchanges that do not deliver these cryptocurrency to companies who are conducting initial coin offerings (ICOs). Typically, the transaction is initiated through online wallets.

Keep current with the progress of the Startup.

Many people invest their money in new businesses and then cross their fingers and hope for the best. Even while there is nothing inherently wrong with doing this, if you want the very best outcomes, you will likely need to put in even more work. Investing in cryptocurrencies is, after all, a very significant undertaking. You should not take things lightly unless you want to risk losing the money you've worked so hard to obtain.

Trading cryptocurrencies is fraught with peril and is mostly a game of chance. As a result, it is prudent to disperse the risks you take. You will have a lower chance of losing if you play in this manner. In addition to that, you need to make a greater effort to learn more about the companies that you are interested in. Take in the latest news. Surf around on the Internet. Engage in conversation with others who share your values and who may be able to provide assistance.

Attending conferences where the team will also be present is another option. Communicate with them. Send them messages through e-mail. Find out what their responses are. Make an effort to get familiar with these individuals since it is possible that they may be able to assist you in some way.

What You Ought to Be Aware Of Concerning ICOs

Floyd "Money" Mayweather made headlines in 2017 for his dominant performance against the MMA phenomConor McGregor. Mayweather was nicknamed "Money." In addition to this, he made waves in the technology industry by promoting the Hubii Network on his Instagram and Twitter accounts, which is an initial coin offering (ICO).

Mayweather, who now refers to himself as Floyd "Crypto" Mayweather, has backed initial coin offerings (ICOs) in the past, so this isn't the first time he's done so. In July of 2017, he worked to spread awareness about the initial coin offering (ICO) for the Stox project, which ultimately was successful in raising more than $30 million during its token sale. (It is important to keep in mind that there are certain distinctions between an initial coin offering

(ICO), a token sale, and a crowdsale. Do some research on the keywords to find out more.)

What exactly is an ICO?

In the same way that an initial public offering (IPO) sells shares of a firm to the general public, an initial coin offering (ICO) also sells ownership stakes in a business. During the initial public offering (IPO), a share of stock will represent a fractional ownership stake in a company. According to the documents provided by the ICO, a crypto coin in an initial coin offering (ICO) symbolizes a certain amount of ownership in pretty much any company effort.

In an initial public offering (IPO), new shareholders place their bets on the possibility that the value of their shares will rise over time. When participating in an initial coin offering (ICO), investors have the expectation that the value of the freshly issued cryptocurrency coin will rise. The most significant distinction is that, at the time of this writing, there are very few laws or regulations that are applicable to initial coin offerings (ICOs). It won't remain the Wild Wild West for much longer since regulators are putting in a lot of effort to get control of the initial coin offering (ICO) market and the cryptocurrency sector. Now is the moment to launch an initial coin offering (ICO) for the currency with your brand name on it if you have been considering doing so.

An initial coin offering (ICO) is comparable in difficulty to that of a Kickstarter project. As a result, it is permissible for it to make unsubstantiated promises about how wonderful the product is or how wise it would be for you to invest in it. There is absolutely nothing preventing the individual or team behind the ICO from just take your money and disappearing into the ether. According to a survey by the Cointelegraph, around 10% of initial coin offerings (ICOs) are fraudulent due to the use of phishing, Ponzi schemes, and other schemes.

How exactly does an ICO function?

When you participate in an initial coin offering (ICO), you are effectively purchasing digital coupons that are produced on a blockchain. These coupons may be traded or held, depending on your preference. Smith + Crown states that some initial coin offerings (ICOs) are issuing "meta-tokens" based on known cryptocurrencies such as Bitcoin, despite the fact that blockchain is an essential component of any ICO.

There Is Without a Doubt a Criminal Component, But... Anyone who recalls the issues that occurred with Mt. Gox is aware that the bitcoin sector is far from being a brand-safe and risk-free enterprise. Smith + Crown observes that many initial coin offerings (ICOs) are advertised as "software presale tokens" (similar to an early access video game on a gaming platform such as Steam), using terms such as "crowdsale" or "donation" (rather than ICO) to avoid complying with regulatory requirements. This absence of regulation and control enables rapid development, pivots, and innovation, but it also puts less knowledgeable investors in the hands of individuals who may engage in illegal activity.

Should you be thinking about starting your own initial coin offering? The name "Palmercoin" has an appealing rhythm to it. But I haven't done it yet for a number of reasons that should be very self-explanatory.

Exchanges OfCryptocurrency To Take Into Consideration

As a result of the meteoric rise in popularity of cryptocurrencies over the course of many years, a plethora of online exchanges have emerged. Finding the correct platform to begin with becomes much more difficult as a result of this, particularly for those who are just starting out. In order to facilitate your search, I have compiled a list of some of the most advantageous trades that are worthy of your attention.

It is strongly recommended that you begin with them so that you can more easily get the hang of investing in cryptocurrencies. You'll find on these pages cryptocurrency exchanges that real people have ranked as among the best available. You will also see those that have been given a rating depending on how easily they can be used and how well they perform. And then there are companies that are head and shoulders above the rest in terms of the level of security they provide and the transaction fees they charge.

1. The Gemini

Its primary function is to facilitate transactions using the cryptocurrencies Ether and Bitcoin. It is a very safe place for doing exchanges. In addition to having controlled standards and capital needs, it also provides a straightforward interface that is easy to use. It performs many of the same activities as a conventional bank and is very liquid, assuring that you will be reimbursed. You are able to exchange both sorts of cryptocurrencies for US dollars here, as well as the other way around.

2. The coinbase.

Because it is used by millions of traders at the moment, Coinbase is presently one of the most popular exchanges that are operational right now. Through the use of this platform, not only newcomers but even more experienced traders are getting in on the action of trading cryptocurrencies. The fact that Coinbase provides a broad array of products and services while yet being simple to use is one of the platform's most appealing features. All of the transactions are protected, and there is even an integrated wallet for you to keep your bitcoins in.

3. The Bitstamp exchange

You have access to one of the first trading platforms that was developed specifically for Bitcoin with Bitstamp. Additionally, it provides Bitcoin storage inside the system while maintaining a high level of use and safety. The fact that all Bitcoins held are covered by insurance is the most attractive feature of the latter option. The help desk is open 24 hours a day, seven days a week.

You are welcome to sign up for a totally free account so that you may start taking part in the transaction. It is incredibly simple to use, and it works quite well.

Cexio, number four.

You now have access to a global cryptocurrency exchange platform if you use Cexio. It is quite simple to engage in transactions on this platform, including the exchange of fiat currency for cryptocurrency and vice versa. It is perfect for both novice traders and those with more expertise. It is a wonderful platform to begin with since it is equipped with tools and functionalities that are simple to use. You will also benefit from Cexio's pricing, which are a near approximation of those found on the market, which is another advantage of utilizing the platform.

5. Poloniex (Pound)

In the world of cryptocurrencies, security is of the utmost significance, and as a cryptocurrency trading platform, Poloniex is obligated to meet users' expectations in this regard. It supports hundreds of different cryptocurrencies and trading pairings, and it provides a set of tools that are accessible to both inexperienced and experienced traders alike. The fact that you can always anticipate closing a trade is one of the many benefits of using this platform.

6. The Kraken.

If the Bitcoin is the digital currency of your choice, then using Kraken as your exchange of choice is the best alternative. It is now one of the biggest sites for trading Bitcoins that is accessible. It even has a partnership with the principal digital bank that deals in cryptocurrency transactions. Despite the fact that its primary function is the trading of Bitcoins, it is also able to handle transactions involving Ether and any number of other cryptocurrencies. Traders in the sector that have more experience tend to use this exchange more often than others.

7. Change your form

There are some exchanges, such as those described before, which make it possible to engage in trading while remaining anonymous. With the assistance of Shapeshift, you won't need an account to engage in simple transactions like this one since you won't need to register for one. If you want to conduct all of your business with cryptocurrency, rather than any other kind of currency, then utilizing this exchange will be in your best interest.

Components Of The Hidden Order.

Because its "hidden" order blocks are developed from a more refined stand point of demand and supply, where we look out for BOS, IMBALANCE, and MITIGATION, Hidden order blocks have also been a lovely field of study. This is one of the reasons why Hidden order blocks have been so popular. I will not go back and discuss them since there are many articles written on these issues, and I also have ebooks written on these topics as well.

HIDDEN ORDER BLOCKS, AN EXAMPLE OF A CHART 15.

According to the picture, the order block that is designated as concealed is not the final red candle before the first move. Instead, it is the wicks of the two green candles that are before the move. These order blocks might be difficult to recognize, yet they are just as effective as the standard order blocks that are visible to our eyes. Let's shift now to a more intimate time frame in order to locate the true order block candle (which will undoubtedly be a red candle prior to the bullish surge).

Let's go on to some better instances that feature BOS, IMBALANCE, and other qualities similar to SMC. If you look at the picture that was just shown, the order block can be seen very clearly as the final red candle before the move up.

 This is simply a straightforward example, however the order block cannot be processed since there is neither a BOS nor an IMBALANCE.

EXAMPLE OF A CHART USING HIDDEN ORDER BLOCKS 16.

As seen in the previous example (number 16), the wicks serve as covert order blocks.

By moving to a more granular time frame, we are now in a position to demonstrate that the previously hidden order block is now visible. The only method to determine whether or not a hidden order block is legitimate is to go to a more granular time frame in order to determine whether or not an order block is really present, which would indicate that the hidden order block is legitimate. Let's keep back testing and checking for more examples to see how effective this is and how price reacts to hidden order blocks; from the previous examples, we can see how price reacted to them since they are still order blocks; the only difference is that they are hidden on the bigger time frame. If you don't know about this, you miss the movement, especially if you are a trader who focuses on the bigger time frame.

Exhibit 16.

You don't have to wait for the regular OB to be neutralized once you have acquired confirmation off the hidden OB, which is another benefit of the hidden OB. This is because the normal OB doesn't affect the hidden OB. Exactly the same as what we have above.

Although the OB was concealed on the one-hour time frame, there were still two OBs present here: the hidden OB and the regular OB. You may wish to find out which one is the stronger option. My response is that "once you can spot the order block, at mitigation, you enter off the order block which meets your entry parameters either wyckoff or whatever else you are using." This is what I mean by "once you can spot the order block."

You would have drawn out the normal order block if you hadn't seen the hidden OB, and once it didn't get mitigated, you would have thought something along the lines of "I knew it, my order blocks don't play out, urgh, I quit trading SMC, I need a better strategy!!!" However, because you didn't understand the concept that some order blocks are hidden, you missed the opportunity to get involved in the delivery of price.

The Downsides Of Using Cryptocurrency

Activity in the shadow economy is made easier by a lack of regulation.

The capacity of cryptocurrency to encourage illegal activity is perhaps the most significant disadvantage of the asset, as well as a regulatory worry. Bitcoin and other cryptocurrencies are often used as payment methods in online transactions that take place in the gray and black markets. For example, before it was taken down in 2014, the notorious "dark web" marketplace known as Silk Road was using Bitcoin to make it easier for users to engage in illegal activities such as buying drugs and engaging in other forms of criminal behavior. In addition, cryptocurrencies are becoming an increasingly popular tool for money laundering, which refers to the process of concealing the origin of money by passing it via a purportedly "clean" third party.

Although it should be noted that the founder of Silk Road is now doing time in prison as a result of a years-long investigation by the DEA, the same "strength" that makes it difficult for governments to seize and trace cryptocurrencies also makes it relatively easy for criminals to operate using cryptocurrencies.

There is a Risk of Avoiding Taxes in Certain Countries or States

Because national governments do not regulate cryptocurrencies, and because cryptocurrencies often operate outside of their direct control, cryptocurrencies naturally attract those who want to avoid paying taxes. Many small companies pay their employees in bitcoin and other cryptocurrencies in order to avoid responsibility for payroll taxes and to assist their employees in avoiding liability for income taxes. At the same time, many online sellers accept cryptocurrencies in order to avoid liability for sales taxes and income taxes.

According to the Internal Revenue Service (IRS), the federal government of the United States applies the "same taxation guidelines to all cryptocurrency payment" made by and to people and companies inside the United States. However, a large number of nations do not have policies like these in place. And because of the inherent anonymity of cryptocurrencies, it is difficult to track down tax law violations, especially those using pseudonymous online sellers (in contrast to an employer that publishes an employee's true name on a W-2 form indicating their bitcoin earnings for the tax year).

Possibility of Financial Gain Loss Because of the Data Load

Early supporters of cryptocurrencies felt that digital alternatives to pay held the potential of supporting a shift away from physical cash, which they considered as imperfect and inherently risky. This belief was based on the assumption that digital alternatives to cash could be effectively safeguarded. It is safer to store money in the cloud or even a physical data storage device than it is to keep it in a back pocket or purse, assuming a practically uncrackable source code, an impenetrable authentication protocol (key), and adequate hacker defenses (which Mt. Gox lacked).

On the other hand, this presupposes that users of cryptocurrencies take adequate safety measures to protect their data. For example, users who have stored their private keys on a single physical storage device can suffer irreparable financial loss if the device is misplaced or stolen. This is because the user will no longer have access to their private keys. Even users who save their data with a single cloud service run the risk of losing everything if the server suffers physical damage or becomes disconnected from the global Internet. This is a concern for servers situated in nations with strict Internet control, such as China.

The possibility of substantial price fluctuations and manipulation

A large number of cryptocurrencies have a disproportionately small number of outstanding units, which are held by a small group of individuals (typically the currency's creator and other associated parties). The holders of the currency essentially control the supply of the currency, which makes it susceptible to extreme value swings and outright manipulation — in a manner similar to that of thinly traded penny stocks.

It Is Commonly Unpossible to Trade Cryptocurrencies for Fiat money In general, only the most widely used cryptocurrencies, or those that have the highest market capitalization as measured in dollars, have specialized online exchanges that allow for the direct trade of cryptocurrencies for fiat money. The ret do not have their own dedicated online exchange, and hence cannot be directly traded in for fiat currency at this time. Instead, users are required to first change their holdings into a cryptocurrency that is more widely used, such as Bitcoin, before they may convert their holdings into fiat currency. This "upprees demand for," and hence the value of, certain of the cryptocurrencies that are used for lending.

Although cryptocurrency miners perform the function of a quasi-intermediary during cryptocurrency transactions, they are not responsible for mediating disputes between parties involved in such transactions. The chargeback and refund facilities offered by cryptocurrency miners are limited to nonexistent. In point of fact, the whole idea of such an arbitrator runs counter to the decentralizing imperative that lies at the center of contemporary bitcoin philosophy. If you are cheated in a cryptocurrency transaction — for example, if you pay in advance for an item that you never get - you have no one to turn to since there is no central authority overseeing cryptocurrency transactions. Even while several newer cryptocurrencies make an effort to address the chargeback/refund issue, the solutions to this problem are still insufficient and mostly untested.

Traditional payment methods, such as Visa, Mastercard, and PayPal, on the other hand, are often involved in the resolution of disputes between buyers and sellers. Their procedures on refunds and chargebacks are designed with the specific intent of preventing buyer fraud.

Instead Of Bucking The Trend, Ride It Out.

One of the primary tenets of technical analysis is that before acting on a signal, one must first watch for confirmation that the signal is accurate. Do not try to be clever by attempting to estimate where the precise bottom is located. Instead, you should wait for a reversal to clearly define itself before deploying your assets so that you may capitalize on the new trend while it is still in its early stages.

How can we tell when we've reached rock bottom? What signs should we look for to determine whether or not that trend has begun to reverse? In the first place, you need to be on the lookout for a rise in the volume. When bulls and bears are engaged in a tug of war over who will dominate the momentum of the market, the volume of trade tends to be highest at the extremes of the chart.

If the market is moving in a downward direction, you will be able to recognize a falling resistance trend that may be used to gauge the size of any future rebound. You may make a note of such levels and utilize them as possible turning points for momentum as the price will produce a succession of lower highs on attempted rebound.

If you are prepared to be vigilant and seek for indications in the price movement, momentum will reveal itself to you in a manner that is plain and unmistakable.

The formation of a higher low is the true first step towards producing any sustained rebound and is likely the factor that is most critical to any prospective reversal.

A psychological explanation may be provided for the formation of a higher low. Our greed will begin to manifest itself as soon as we come to the conclusion that the bottom has been reached. We hope that the price will fall to that lowest point once again so that we may load, but this time we will do so with the knowledge that the trend is moving in our favor. As the price approaches that lower region once again, market players get worried. Out of worry that they may lose out on an opportunity, they boost their bids higher, and a higher low eventually occurs.

"My greatest piece of advise is to ride the wave of momentum. Don't attempt to be too clever by predicting when it will start moving in the other direction.

Are CryptoKitties allowed under the law?

Yes, it is entirely permissible to own a CryptoKitty, and the blockchain network that they operate on makes it possible for them to do so without violating any laws. Because the United States Securities and Exchange Commission (SEC) has determined that they are an investment asset, anybody who wants to buy one must be at least 18 years old. Because of this, it is against the law for anybody less than 18 years old to purchase a CryptoKitty. In addition to this, the purchase of one of these Kitties is prohibited for anybody who does not have access to their own private key (and the Kitty that is linked with it) in any capacity. Make certain that the recipient is at least 18 years old before giving them a Kitty as a present; otherwise, you might be breaking the law.

Hidden Artwork

Decentralization is the most important concept in cryptography. It is a kind of technology that is gradually becoming more prevalent in our day-to-day activities. And what exactly is meant by the term "decentralized technology"? The answer to that question is, to put it mildly, not always straightforward. On the other hand, we may consider it to be anything that does not have a centralized authority or a governing body. To put it another way, it is a form of technology that does not belong to a certain corporation or group but rather to the general public.

When we keep all of this in mind, it is not hard to see how the idea of NFTs might make sense within the context of the cryptocurrency industry. If you are new to the cryptocurrency sector, it is possible that you are unaware of what NFTs are.

What exactly is the Crypto art?

In a nutshell, Crypto Art is the point where the blockchain industry and the art world converge. In a sense that is more technical, it is a sort of digital asset that is one of a kind and can be purchased and sold on numerous exchanges that deal in cryptocurrencies.

The first work of cryptographic artwork is known as CryptoKitties. It is possible to buy and sell these virtual cats, and there are only a certain number available. On the other hand, the production of these kittens is not constrained by any particular guidelines or regulations. Each one is one of a kind and may be held by either a single person or a group of individuals.

These digital assets are comparable to stocks in that they have ownership and value; yet, they are also distinctive in that there is no predetermined process that specifies how many will be generated or how many there will be overall. This makes it impossible to predict either number. The production of these kittens is not governed by any centralized norms, regulations, or regulatory agencies.

Digital artists from every corner of the globe are now producing one-of-a-kind works of crypto art. This sector of the blockchain ecosystem is poised to become one of the most interesting in the not too distant future. You can purchase and sell digital artwork on a variety of sites, such as OpenSea and RareBits, which are just two examples.

How do you do business with NFTs?

Although crypto art is still in its infancy, this does not imply that there are no avenues through which it may be purchased or sold. The purchasing and selling of digital artwork is often done via the use of decentralized exchanges. These exchanges operate in a manner comparable to that of stock exchanges; yet, their structures are far more flexible and distinctive.

Additionally, crypto art is used by a lot of individuals as a type of investment. They saw it not just as a potential route to financial success, but also as an opening to assist musicians from all over the globe. These artists are producing stunning pieces of art, which are then being purchased and sold on a daily basis. There have even been sales of crypto art for millions of dollars for individual works! This is an exciting moment for crypto art, and we can only anticipate that this dynamic business will continue to wow us in the years to come.

How The Technology Behind Blockchain Works

The blockchain technology is really a simplification of three separate but related technologies. These are as follows:

The art of ciphering

Security cryptography based on a distributed network that incentivizes record keeping

People who use the blockchain technology are each provided with two cryptographic keys—a private key and a public key—with which they are able to conduct commercial transactions.

A trustworthy identification reference may be built with the help of these two keys. On the blockchain network, each participant is able to be uniquely recognized by using a combination of their private key and public key.

If I wish to do business, I will need to use both my public key, which is my bitcoin address, and my private key, which serves as both my password and my authentication mechanism. If I do not use both of these, I will not be able to do so.

Network that is Distributed

Because there is no central bank, cashier, or anybody else whose duty it is to verify, control, and confirm transactions, a distributed network system is used instead. This system allows anyone to join and begin monitoring transactions that take place on the network.

Therefore, as soon as two cryptographic keys are combined to symbolize that a person needs to conduct a transaction (they take their private key, and combine it with the public key), an announcement of some sort is made, and a block consisting of a digital signature, time stamp, and any other pertinent information is generated. This block is then broadcast across the network to all of the nodes in the network.

At this point, the question of whether or not there should be incentives for retaining records arises.

Why would anybody be interested in merely sitting down to watch transactions on the block chain network; don't they have jobs to complete? Why would anyone want to do that? Have you have a life to go to?

The individuals who are responsible for monitoring the transactions that take place on the blockchain network do not do so without compensation; rather, they do it as part of a process known as mining.

The Fifth Chapter Teaches You How to Make Use of Cryptocurrencies

Hundreds of thousands of merchants and sellers operating in a wide variety of markets are beginning to acknowledge cryptocurrencies as a legitimate payment option as cryptocurrency's popularity continues to rise. There has been a recent uptick in the number of individuals purchasing cryptocurrencies. Additionally, governments are starting to take notice of cryptocurrencies. Bitcoin has just recently been acknowledged as a legitimate currency by the Japanese government. This demonstrates that if you haven't already done so, it is only a matter of time until you will be able to use cryptocurrencies to pay for a service such as your home utilities.

The process of paying for a product or service with a cryptocurrency is analogous to writing and sending an email. The one and only distinction is that with cryptocurrency, rather of sending a message to a person's email address, you send money to their bitcoin wallet address. With email, you send a message to a person's email address. When you pay for products and services using bitcoin, you are forced to divulge very little to no personal information, depending on what it is that you are buying for. This is the primary advantage of utilizing cryptocurrency. For instance, if you are making a payment for a physical goods, the only information that is needed is your name and address, since they are required for the purposes of mailing the thing. If you are purchasing a digital item, all you have to do is pay for it and download it; you do not need to provide any other information. The only information that other sellers will want from you is your email address.

If you choose to pay for your purchase with bitcoin, rather of being asked for your credit card number during the checkout process, you will see the merchant's cryptocurrency payment details displayed there instead. This will either be a QR code, the address of your cryptocurrency wallet, or a link depending on the kind of cryptocurrency wallet you are using. If the retailer has provided their wallet address, all that is required of you is to copy the address, paste it into your own wallet, input the amount that needs to be paid, and then make the payment.

The vast majority of retailers that accept cryptocurrency payments will include a QR code on the checkout page for customers' convenience and to make payments more straightforward. Paying using your mobile device in a method that is both very fast and simple thanks to QR codes. When you scan the QR code with your smart phone, you will get an address of a cryptocurrency wallet along with the amount that has to be paid into your own wallet. This information is going to be prefilled for you automatically on your wallet. To finish the transaction, all you need to do at that point is hit the transmit button on your computer.

A Coinbase wallet provides even another convenient option for paying using bitcoin, which can be used to purchase products and services. Because the vast majority of businesses who do business in bitcoin utilize Coinbase, the entire procedure may be simplified by utilizing Coinbase. The process of making a payment using Coinbase is simplified when you are making purchases from a retailer that utilizes the platform. You will just need to confirm your purchase from inside your Coinbase account in order to bring the checkout process to a successful conclusion. Your payment will be immediately communicated to the seller when it has been processed.

It may be simple and handy to make purchases with cryptocurrencies, but what exactly can be paid for with these virtual currencies? Where can you use the bitcoin that you have? You will be pleased to know that there are a few locations where you may make payments using bitcoin. In the early days of bitcoin, these early forms of digital cash were only used on the dark web. They were avoided by most of the merchants. There were just a few retailers that were technologically adept enough to accept bitcoin payments. Things are different now than they were before. Several businesses and merchants now accept cryptocurrency payments. This figure is only going to grow up as more people become aware of how cryptocurrencies function and get a knowledge of how they operate. The following categories of establishments now accept bitcoin as a form of payment:

Internet-based merchants: There are now several hundred online stores that enable users to pay for products and services with cryptocurrency. These merchants have made this option available to their customers. Microsoft, The Gap, WordPress, Tesla, Bloomberg, Overstock, Tiger Direct, Zynga, and Dell are just few of the companies that fall within this category. There are many more. Because it is the most extensively used cryptocurrency, Bitcoin is also the cryptocurrency that is accepted by the greatest number of online shops. Nevertheless, a few of these merchants will also take other forms of cryptocurrency for payment.

Traditional storefront retailers: The traditional brick-and-mortar stores have not been forgotten. CeX and REEDS Jewelers are two examples of well-known brick-and-mortar businesses that welcome customers paying using bitcoin. Bitcoin is now accepted as a form of payment for event tickets by a number of major sports clubs, including the Sacramento Kings and the San Jose Earthquakes, among others. Even payment for medical services at the Medicover Group Hospital may be made using bitcoin if you want to do so.

Do you like the concept of utilizing cryptocurrencies to pay for various aspects of your holiday, such as flights and hotels? One Shot Hotels, Expedia, CheapAir, The Holiday Inn in Brooklyn, AirLituanica, and AirBaltic are just few of the well-known names in the travel industry that accept cryptocurrencies as payment. Other firms that do so include AirBaltic and AirLituanica. Even payments for space travel may be made with cryptocurrencies via Virgin Galactic.

In spite of the fact that they are digital currency, cryptocurrencies have the potential to be transformed into tangible assets. For example, Amagi Metals enables customers to trade their bitcoins for physical gold bullion. You can buy a property using bitcoin by going to mycoinrealty.com and making your purchase there. Tesla Motors allows customers to pay in cryptocurrencies for the purchase of its electric vehicles.

Transfer of funds and remittances: Cryptocurrencies like as Ripple provide a worldwide real-time settlement system that makes it possible to send and receive money quickly across international borders. When compared to more traditional methods such as bank transfers and services provided by companies like Western Union, using bitcoin to conduct international money transfers offers a number of benefits. People may avoid the unfavorable exchange rates and large transfer fees paid by banks by transferring relatively modest sums of money using cryptocurrencies, which is particularly beneficial when sending relatively small amounts of money. Cryptocurrencies also are much faster than banks. The processing time for a Bitcoin transfer is around ten minutes, but it might take a bank anywhere from one to three days to validate a transaction. Although money transfer services like Western Union are exactly as quick, the fees they charge are orders of magnitude more. Some systems, such as CoinPip, make it possible for businesses to make payments to distant contractors and merchants using cryptocurrencies. The payments are sent to the suppliers in their own country's currency, and the corporation is spared the expense of paying the exorbitant bank fees.

gaming: There are gaming sites that take cryptocurrency, such as PeerBet, Primedice, and SatoshiDice, for those people who are interested in the idea of converting their cryptocurrency coins into even more cryptocurrency coins via the process of gambling. Some casino operators, such as VikingSlots, are exploring the possibilities presented by blockchain technology in an effort to discover methods by which they can ensure the fairness of their games.

Services of a broad kind: Numerous companies that provide services of a general nature have begun accepting cryptocurrencies as a form of payment. You may use bitcoin to pay for subscriptions to services like OkCupid and Treehouse, as well as certain VPN providers, and you can even use it to pay for work on Fiverr. You can purchase domain names and web hosting on Namecheap using cryptocurrency. Bitcoin has just been accepted for use as a method of payment for a variety of costs, including tuition, at the University of Nicosia, which is located in Cyprus.

Gift cards: eGifter, GiftCardZen, Gyft, and iTradeBTC are just few of the gift card firms that accept bitcoin payments among their customer base. After purchasing a gift card from one of these firms, the card may then be used at well-known stores such as Amazon, Walmart, Target, and Nike to make purchases. The one and only disadvantage of doing so is that you could wind up paying a greater price for the gift cards than you would if you had purchased them using conventional currency.

Donating to your favorite charitable organizations is another option open to you while using cryptocurrency. Donations of cryptocurrencies may be sent to nonprofit organizations such as Sean's Outposts and Sri Lanka Campaign for Peace and Justice. Donations in the form of cryptocurrencies may also be sent to other users within the Reddit community by users of the platform.

When it comes to the adoption of cryptocurrencies, gaming and e-sports firms have not been left in the dust as other industries have been. A growing number of gaming firms now accept cryptocurrency payments from clients for the purchase of video games. Users of games published by other firms are given the option of paying for in-game items using cryptocurrency currencies. Players may even use bitcoin to gamble on themselves in competitions by putting a bounty that other players can collect in the event that they kill them in-game. This bounties can be collected in the event that players use cryptocurrency to purchase an item.

Numerous other tiny stores numbering in the hundreds: There has been a meteoric rise in both the use of and interest in virtual currencies in recent years. You may be able to uncover a number of other establishments that take cryptocurrencies depending on the region in where you currently are located. Each day, a great number of new companies, both online and offline, join the movement. It is just a matter of time until the majority of businesses throughout the globe accept cryptocurrencies as a form of payment.

Notable Cryptocurrencies Apart From BitcoinAndEthereum

There are over 800 different cryptocurrencies as of the time this article was written, and there are virtually weekly announcements of new initial coin offerings. Even while it may be difficult for any compendium of cryptocurrencies to include everything, there are surely certain cryptocurrencies that are worthy of being included in some capacity, even if they do not merit their own entire chapter. This chapter provides a list of more cryptocurrencies that are noteworthy either because of their historical relevance, their ambition, their ingenuity, or just because of their eccentricity.

The Z-Cash (ZEC)

Zcash is yet another cryptocurrency that places a significant emphasis on maintaining users' privacy. It has a predetermined maximum of twenty-one million coins, much as Bitcoin does, but its mining algorithm was intended to offer home-based miners with ordinary computers a chance to mine. This makes the process more democratic and decentralized than Bitcoin mining, which has a limited maximum of only twenty-one million coins. To put it another way, it is a cryptocurrency that combines Dash and Litecoin.

In September of 2016, Zooko Wilcox-Ohearn presented Zcash with the intention of expanding upon the previous work done by cryptography academics at Johns

Hopkins University and other institutions. Since 2014, the researchers have been hard at work on a privacy mechanism that they called Zerocoin. The development of Zcash was the inevitable consequence of the study.

The particular mechanisms by which Zcash achieves its goal of maintaining users' anonymity are quite resilient and rather difficult to describe. Zcash, in its most basic form, employs zero-knowledge proofs as a means of concealing the identity of both the sender and the receiver of a transaction, in addition to the total value of the transaction. It is beyond the scope of this book to explain zero-knowledge proofs; nonetheless, the final result is that anonymity is achieved by making the sending and receiving address any random address on the blockchain itself. This is quite similar to the mixing idea that was mentioned before. Zcash, much like Dash, provides its users with the choice to make their address information available to the public if they so want.

After only one year, Zcash has established itself as a leading cryptocurrency. It has consistently maintained a position inside the top 20 most valuable cryptocurrencies, as ranked by market capitalization. Despite the fact that the blockchain is open to the public, it provides a level of anonymity that is comparable to that provided by Monero, which will be covered in a later section.

The website for Zcash is z.cash.

The Dogecoin symbol, DOGE

Dogecoin was many people's first experience with alternative cryptocurrencies as well as their most entertaining one. An image of a happy ShibaInu dog with misspelled Comic Sans lettering superimposed on top of it serves as the inspiration for the cryptocurrency known as Dogecoin (or "DOGE"). Despite the fact that Dogecoin was first created as a joke, its original programmer had the goal of developing a cryptocurrency that would be more accessible to a wider audience than Bitcoin by having a humorous tone. In addition, the creation of Dogecoin was an effort to improve the image of Bitcoin, which had been tainted by its association with darknet markets such as the Silk Road and Alphabay, which offered illicit narcotics, pornography, and other illegal products and services. The development of Dogecoin was an attempt to rectify this association.

Since Dogecoin and Litecoin both employ the Scrypt algorithm, it is impossible to manufacture specialised mining machines for either cryptocurrency. However, this does not prevent anybody from mining Dogecoin. Dogecoin's block time is much lower than that of Litecoin's, which implies that its blocks are validated considerably more quickly. In addition to this, it employs a distinct mining block difficulty algorithm from that of Litecoin, which was designed with the express purpose of discouraging the use of mining pools.

The formal launch of Dogecoin occurred in December of 2013, and the cryptocurrency had a significant price increase during the first three days of its existence. After this momentary boost in popularity, the value decreased by 80% as a result of the increased number of enthusiasts who began to take advantage of how simple it was to mine the fledgling currency.

The most common usage for dogecoin these days is as a kind of online gratuity. However, the Dogecoin community as well as the Dogecoin Foundation have emerged as key forces in the world of fundraising. Dogecoin initiatives have funded the participation of a bobsled team in the Winter Olympics as well as the construction of wells in Kenya as part of the Doge4Water initiative.

Dogecoin.com is the domain name of the cryptocurrency's main website. You will discover what is without a doubt the catchiest and most memorable introduction films of any cryptocurrency on that website.

Buying Things From Local Businesses

Buying Bitcoins locally, in person, is the second way to acquire them in return for the usage of fiat cash. This may be done either online or offline. When opposed to utilizing an exchange, employing this approach enables you to get a price that is somewhat more favorable. Another benefit of making a purchase locally is that it is handy for users who are located in countries that do not have easy access to internet exchanges since they are able to quickly acquire coins in person. This is because users in these countries may purchase coins in a straightforward manner. In terms of safety, escrow services safeguard financial transactions from being fraudulently completed.

How to Securely Store YourBitcoins

Now that you have your first Bitcoins, the next question you should ask yourself is how to keep them safe. You have the option of moving your Bitcoin away from the exchange and into a Bitcoin wallet, which operates in the same manner as a traditional wallet. You will be able to determine how many bitcoins are currently stored in your wallet, and you will also be able to use it to spend your bitcoin. It is essential to bear in mind that your wallet does not, in and of itself, hold your Bitcoin due to the decentralized nature of Bitcoin and the fact that it is held on the Blockchain.

Depending on the exchange, such as Coinbase, you may be able to get a wallet; however, day trading prevents this. However, experienced traders recommend that newcomers withdraw their coins from the exchange as a precautionary measure since it is possible for exchanges to be hacked. If you move your money to your Bitcoin wallet, they will be stored in a more secure location. It is a possibility. For instance, in 2011 the Bitcoin exchange Mt. Gox, which is situated in Tokyo and was the victim of a cyberattack, had losses of 27 million dollars. Because to this, a total of 460 million dollars' worth of Bitcoin was lost among their 80,000 members.

It is necessary to point out that the cryptocurrency exchange known as Mt. Gox is not a "fly-by-night" operation. It housed the most extensive cryptocurrency exchange in the history of the globe. On the other hand, their security processes were lacking, which made them an easy target. In the midst of charges of fraud, the cryptocurrency exchange Mt. Gox finally filed a bankruptcy petition. The majority of the coins that were taken were never found again. Therefore, if you want to ensure the safety of your Bitcoins, you need choose a secure storage facility. This is the only way to guarantee their protection.

The following is a selection of the Bitcoin wallets that are available to you:

Wallets for your desktop

When you want to move your Bitcoins off of an exchange, using them is a straightforward option. When you use a digital wallet, you do not need to carry extra information with you as you do when using a paper or hardware wallet. A desktop wallet may be thought of as a virtual bank account that stores bitcoins on your own computer. The vast majority of these desktop wallets have encryption, which ensures the safety of your private key, which is a string of between 26 and 35 alphabetic and numeric characters that serves as your wallet address.

Some examples of desktop wallets are as follows:

A piece of electrum

Because Electrum's source code is freely available to the public, there is a much reduced risk that its creators may unintentionally introduce a vulnerability. It gives you the ability to store and spend your Bitcoins in an easy and accessible manner. You have the option of storing your private keys in an offline location and going online in a "watching only" mode, which will protect your money in the event that your computer is compromised. Additionally, it is compatible with a variety of hardware wallets.

The Exodus

However, Exodus is not an open-source project. However, in addition to Bitcoin, it is also capable of storing other cryptocurrencies such as Litecoin, Ethereum, and Dogecoin. It has a user interface that is easier to navigate than Electrum.

To Pay

Both your desktop computer and your mobile device may be used to make payments using CoPay. To verify your account and spend your money, it requires numerous signatures from different people. There is also an option for multiple users, which means you may give it to other members of your family to utilize. It has a code source that is free to the public.

It is essential to keep in mind that desktop wallets may only be used if your personal computer is connected to the internet; as a result, these wallets are susceptible to being hacked.

The Blockchain Technology And An Explanation Of How It Functions

The Blockchain Technology is a kind of technology that helps to make it easier to transfer digital information across different networks. Imagine the blockchain technology as a shared database or spreadsheet that each member of your family keeps on their own personal computer.

Let's say you were still a teenager when your father developed a spreadsheet file and placed it on the computers of every member of the family so that everyone in the family, who shares a common bank account, could submit their weekly spending plans and budgets. You and your siblings have to post all of the transactions that you made with your daily pocket money at the end of each day so that the rest of the family may see how you spent it.

Because your parents are able to simply see whatever you add to the spreadsheet, there is no need for you to communicate anything to them about it. They just need to glance at the spreadsheet, regardless of whether they are in Australia, Japan, or at home, in order to know when you need additional pocket money.

Dad is aware of the times when mum needs financial assistance for going food shopping and when it is time to pay the bills for the household utilities. Because there is no need for anybody to provide information orally, the system continues to function properly even if you attend a college that is located in a different state. The blockchain technology functions in the same manner; it may be thought of as a digital ledger that has been cloned numerous times across a network.

The information that is uploaded into the network is referred to as blocks; whenever new information is uploaded into the network, it will be claimed that a new block has been added to the previous chain of blocks; this is how the term blockchain came to be used to refer to the chain of blocks.

The information that is kept on the blockchain network is not kept in a single place or database, and it is not under the control of a single individual. Instead, it is kept on several computers that are spread out over the globe and are referred to as nodes. These nodes are accountable for establishing new blocks on the chain and keeping the network's information up to date with newly discovered data.

Cryptography is another component that underpins the operation of the blockchain technology. Cryptography is a technique that encrypts information by converting it into a series of codes before it is either stored or sent. This ensures that only those who are permitted to do so are able to decipher the information.

On the blockchain network, information is provided in the form of a collection of codes and numbers. Because of this, it is impossible to determine who began a specific transaction, how many bitcoins a user has, or with whom they are doing business.

You are able to conduct commercial transactions in complete secrecy thanks to the blockchain technology.

In this manner, the transactions that take place on the blockchain network are completed.

The creation of your digital bitcoin wallet will result in the generation of two sets of keys for you to use going forward: a private key and a public key. Consider the public key to be the equivalent of your account number since it serves as your identification on the network. A private key will also be sent to you. This is your password, which is very crucial for the authorisation process. It is impossible for transactions to take place on the blockchain network unless these two keys are coupled.

When you need to carry out a transaction on the network, for example, when you need to pay Mr. X for the items that you purchased from him, you need to take your private keys and public keys and then combine them. This sends signals to the blockchain network that a transaction is going to take place, and it is necessary for you to do this before you can carry out the transaction. The system performs authorization and authentication checks to ensure that you are the one who authorized the transaction and that you have sufficient bitcoin to cover the amount you want to transfer. It also verifies that you are the one who authorized the transaction.

Following this, a block will be produced. This block stores all of the transaction data in an encrypted form, including a time stamp and digital signature. This block is a part of the blockchain. The transaction is completed successfully, but there are no bank tellers or clerks available to record the details of the exchange. As a result, the task of recording transactions on the distributed digital ledger maintained by the blockchain falls to the linked nodes on the network.

People just like you and me, who have offered their time to keep the transactions on the blockchain network up to current, make up these nodes.

They serve in an unofficial capacity as the bank tellers for the blockchain network.

Therefore, whenever a transaction takes place, they are required to update the ledger; but, in order for that to take place, they will first be shown a series of mathematical equations that they will need to find solutions for. The transaction block will not be added to the block unless this mathematical equation is first solved, at which point it will be added.

This Is The Main Library Window, Sometimes Known As The Gui.

You will be taken to the main application window as soon as the welcome wizard has finished processing your information. I'd want to draw your attention to a few different aspects of this, thank you very much. The book list is the most important component. This occupies the most of the window and sets out the books on a table in an organized fashion. The search bar is located just above the book list, and just above that is the tool bar. We will discuss the search bar in more detail later. A 'Device' icon will appear next to the 'Library' symbol in the tool bar as soon as you connect a compatible e-book reader to your computer. By clicking on the symbols that correspond to your e-book reader and your library, you will be able to flip between seeing books that are stored in either location.

The panel that runs down the right side of the window displays information about the book that is presently chosen, including a picture of the book's cover. If you double click anywhere in the detail section, even on the book cover itself, a new window will open and provide further information about the book. If you click on any of the blue text in this section, you will trigger an action that is relevant to the content. To give you an example, if you click the author's name, your web browser will open and a Wikipedia search will be performed for information on the author.

There are four icons and the phrase "Jobs" located at the bottom right hand corner of the window. When one of these icons is clicked, the corresponding view state in the GUI will be toggled. In order, starting from the left:

The tag on the baggage may be used to toggle the tag browser, which is located on the left side of the window. More will be spoken about this at a later time.

The cover flow display may be toggled with the curved arrow. Cover flow organizes the book covers in a sequence that is analogous to the way a juke box presents an album's track listing. The cover of the chosen book is shown in the middle, while those of the other books are angled to the side. You may browse through the book covers by using the left and right arrow buttons on your keyboard to go from one to the next. The book list will continue to be seen underneath the flow area for the covers.

The cover grid view may be toggled using the nine squares in a grid. The book list has been replaced by a grid of book covers thanks to the cover grid. You may want to consider this from the perspective of a bookcase.

The book allows the reader to change whether or not the details panel on the right is shown.

One of the most important components of the graphical user interface is the indication for the tasks. The text "Jobs:," the number that is directly next to it, and the circular progress indicator are all shown here. The circular icon will spin whenever calibre is doing some action (conversion, transferring books to the reader, downloading news, etc.), and the number that appears in the center will indicate the number of tasks (activities) that calibre is now carrying out. You may see additional information about the jobs that are currently being worked on by clicking any portion of the jobs indication.

Finally, if you do not want to keep hold of your Bitcoin (for example, if your suppliers and landlord need payment in fiat currency), these kinds of processors are able to rapidly change your money into fiat currency.

Advertise the acceptance of Bitcoin.

It is quite helpful to indicate to your customers that you do, in fact, accept Bitcoin. Your customers will appreciate this very much. If you have an online storefront, you should get a banner that says

"BitcoinAccepted Here" and post it on your website just below the buttons for PayPal, MasterCard, Visa, and any other payment methods you already provide.

If you run a traditional brick-and-mortar business, you can get up stickers like this for your front door or cash register right here.

Keeping Books and Doing Taxes

Make contact with your accountant in order to determine how to properly keep records of Bitcoin transactions. There are starting to be some accounting firms that focus on Bitcoin and other cryptocurrencies. These firms are beginning to emerge.

WHY SHOULD YOU BEGIN TO ACCEPT BITCOIN AS PAYMENT?

The primary reason why companies are beginning to accept Bitcoin as a form of payment is as follows:

Reduced costs of transactions: Bitcoin has the potential to bring credit card processing rates down to less than 1 percent.

No Chargebacks: Because Bitcoin transactions cannot be reversed, this feature automatically eliminates the possibility of a chargeback or return occurring, as is the case with credit card purchases.

The International Facilitation Organization The transfer of: Avoiding sales is something that many local internet retailers and other types of businesses do. and internationally because of the high costs associated with transacting across international borders. Bitcoin eases the burden of the high fees associated with international transactions by facilitating transactions that are not only quicker but also less expensive.

Fraud Prevention: Bitcoin offers a level of security against identity theft that credit cards and other banking services are simply unable to give. This is because Bitcoin uses cryptography to verify transactions. Once payment has been made to you, there is no longer any chance that it will be contested.

Payouts made more quickly and at a lower cost: For many small businesses, the ability to access funds quickly is very necessary to ensure their continued existence. If you accept Bitcoin as payment, you will have immediate access to the funds, which is far sooner than when using a credit card to make a purchase.

Purchase Your First Coins From A Cryptocurrency Exchange.

After you have created a cryptocurrency wallet — the kind of wallet you use will be determined by the digital currency you ultimately decide to invest in — the next step is to visit an exchange so that you may purchase some coins.

Only a select few of the many available exchanges will allow you to exchange your fiat currency for Bitcoins or any other cryptocurrency you intend to purchase. This is to say that only a select few exchanges accept the use of Visa, MasterCard, or credit cards to purchase cryptocurrencies. This is an important point to keep in mind because it is relevant to the discussion at hand.

Bitcoin is the currency you should purchase first because it is the most popular and many exchanges enable you to use it to buy other tokens. This is an important point to keep in mind since it is the coin you should buy first because it is the most popular. In addition to this, the vast majority of cryptocurrency exchanges are not required to comply with any regulatory requirements, which makes purchasing cryptocurrency from them a risky endeavor; be aware of this fact.

Because cryptocurrency exchanges deal in virtual currencies rather than conventional stocks, unlike traditional stock exchanges, they do not shut nor have opening and closing hours; rather, they are open 24 hours a day, 365 days a year. This is one of the many advantages of cryptocurrency exchanges.

The following are some of the most prominent exchanges on which users may purchase and sell cryptocurrencies:

Website: coinbase.com

The website CoinMama.com.

The website Kraken.com

The Gemini.com

The website LocalBitcoins.com

Bitcoin.com'sBitcoin Wallet

The Cex.io

Bitstamp.net is the website.

Step 3: Engage in Various Trades

The next thing you need to know, now that you have a solid grasp of how wallets and exchanges function, is how trading works so that in the end, if you decide to trade or sell the few coins you have acquired, you will know what to do and how to go about doing it.

The first thing you need to realize is that most exchanges use a trading platform that is quite similar to one another, despite the fact that each exchange is unique. Because the majority of exchanges use the same trading pairings, it can be said that the vast majority of exchanges only trade tokens against Bitcoin, with a few exceptions where they also trade tokens against Ethereum.

This is due, in part, to the fact that bitcoins, in comparison to other cryptocurrencies, have the highest degree of divisibility; one bitcoin may be broken down into 10 million smaller units. See the graphic below for a more detailed explanation of this. This essentially implies that you do not have to acquire or sell a whole Bitcoin when transacting with it. You have the ability to purchase and sell portions of your Bitcoin holdings in exchange for other cryptocurrencies.

When you trade, you should refer to the value of your trades in terms of Bitcoin rather than the value of your country's currency; this is what we mean when we talk about trading pairs. Even though it may take some time to get accustomed to, it is in your best interest to do so. Instead of dealing in your nation's fiat currency, the majority of exchanges use Bitcoin as the trading pair for token transactions and will accept buy and sell orders in relation to Bitcoin.

When it comes to the real business of trading, there are just three things you need to keep in mind:

Restriction of trade: When you engage in limit trading, the system provides you the ability to not only indicate the price at which you want to buy or sell a token but also the quantity of tokens that you want to purchase or sell when the token in question achieves the specified price. Limit trading is a trading technique. This enables you to automate the process of selling and filling orders. For example, if you purchase ten Bitcoins at a price of $8,000 each and then put in a limit trade order to sell all of the coins if and when the price of Bitcoin rises to $20,000 per Bitcoin, the system will carry out your order exactly when the token price rises to the predetermined price.

Trade on the market: You may purchase tokens on certain exchanges, including Binance, for the price that is currently being traded for them on the market. When you need to quickly acquire or sell a token, using this alternative is going to be your best bet. This option is referred to as "Ask" on certain exchanges.

Stop Limit: A stop limit is a kind of trading technique that enables you to activate an order at the moment when the tokens that you have selected to invest in reach a specific price or better. For instance, if you set a stop limit of $10, your computer will begin automatically acquiring token up to the limit that you have set whenever the price of your favorite token is $10 or less. This will continue until the limit that you have set is reached.

Even though there is a lot more to learn about crypto trading, if you can get a handle on these three ideas, you will be well on your way to having a better grasp of how cryptocurrency trading works and how you can get started in it if you do decide to go into it.

The Complete Step-By-Step Guide ToBitcoin Trading For Profit For Novices

Trading bitcoins may be a very lucrative endeavor, both for professionals and novices alike. The market is still relatively new, and its spreads are quite wide. Trading on leverage and engaging in arbitrage are both widely available options. Trading bitcoin thus presents an opportunity for a large number of individuals to generate income.

Bitcoin's history of bubbles and volatility has probably done more than any other aspect of the cryptocurrency to bring in new users and investors. This may be the case more than any other factor.

Every Bitcoin boom generates hysteria, which helps to keep the cryptocurrency's name in the news. The attention that was paid by the media caused more people to get interested, which drove up the price until the hype died down.

Trading using Bitcoin

Each time the price of Bitcoin rises, more investors and speculators want a piece of the profit. Trading in bitcoin is made easy by the fact that the cryptocurrency is used all over the world and can be sent with relative ease.

Trading in bitcoins is quite easy to get started with when compared to trading in other financial assets. Trading may begin very immediately if you already have some bitcoin in your possession. In many instances, verification is not even required in order to engage in business transactions.

If you are interested in trading Bitcoin, there are several online trading businesses that provide the product, which is often referred to as a contract for difference. You may find these organizations by searching the internet.

Bitcoin Is Global Bitcoin is not a fiat currency, which means that the price of Bitcoin is not directly related to the economy of any one country or the policies of that country. Throughout its history, bitcoin's price has responded to a wide variety of events, from China's devaluation of the Yuan to capital restrictions in Greece, among other things. Some of Bitcoin's price spikes have been attributed to widespread economic uncertainty and a sense of impending doom.

Bitcoin Trades Around the Clock

There is no such thing as a "off-exchange" for bitcoin, unlike the stock market. On the contrary, there are hundreds of exchanges all around the world that are open around the clock. Because there is no official Bitcoin exchange, there is also no official Bitcoin price. OfficalBitcoin exchanges do not exist. This may result in the creation of arbitrage possibilities; nevertheless, the majority of the time exchange rates remain within the same general price range.

The price of bitcoin is notoriously volatile due to its penchant for making quick and frequent price shifts.

Discover a Trading Platform As was said previously, there is no official Bitcoin trading platform. Users have various options to choose from, and while making their decision, they should take into account the following considerations:

Regulation and Trust: Can we have confidence in the transaction? Is there a risk that the exchange may make off with customer funds?

Location is essential if you need to deposit fiat cash, and the exchange must be able to process payments originating from your country.

What percentage of each trade constitutes the 'Fee' that is charged?

Large traders will want a Bitcoin exchange that has a high volume of trading activity in addition to a solid level of market depth.

Myths Regarding Non-Fungible Tokens

NFTs and non-fungible tokens have been the subject of a number of misconceptions. This is quite comprehensible when one considers the length of time that the majority of these myths have been around. Listed below is a rundown of some of the most common misconceptions:

Myth: "Ethereum has thousands of pending transactions" is one of the most widespread misunderstandings about Ethereum. This exposes a common misunderstanding about the operation of blockchains and the data processing that they do. There is no correlation between the amount of pending transactions and the number of individuals utilizing the network or the network's level of popularity. It only indicates that there are many transactions in this block that are unsure, which is a good thing considering the number of users and developers who use Ethereum. The value of Ethereum rises according to the number of new users who adopt and make use of it. That may be the case in certain marketplaces, but it certainly isn't the case in the majority of situations.

Myth: "NFTs are a scam" is yet another widespread misunderstanding about NFTs. This was acceptable a few years ago since most people were not aware with the concept of non-fungible tokens at that time. Despite this, the idea eventually faded away as more people gained an understanding of what they were and how they worked. Today, a growing number of seasoned traders who are familiar with the benefits offered by blockchain technology and NFTs are beginning to regard them as investments rather than cons. During 2018, nine percent of all NFTs that were exchanged on the Ethereum network were able to do this.

Another common misunderstanding concerning non-fungible tokens is the

"NFTs are too volatile" myth. The price of an NFT will fluctuate in the same way that the cost of any other currency or token would. This is due to the fact that it is not associated with a certain object and may be used in a variety of different games. For this reason, it may be traded in return for real-world items and virtual games.

Myth: "NFTs are too pricey" — This statement is not at all accurate. The price of NFTs may fluctuate, but on average, they are priced in the same way as other cryptocurrencies, which are already quite low in comparison to normal currencies. This suggests that you are able to acquire an unlimited quantity of NFTs at a price that is far lower than that of traditional money.

Myth: "NFTs are too complex and hard to make" — This is another myth that is not true. Everything hinges on the game developer and the blockchain platform that they choose to use for the game. Because there are several other platforms based on the blockchain, developers may choose whichever one best suits their needs. On the other hand, if they utilize Ethereum, they may use a tool called NFT-Crowdfund to create their very own NFT coin. This indicates that they do not need to become proficient in a separate programming language or construct their own smart contracts in order to produce their NFTs since they can depend on a protocol. They will only want basic information about Ethereum and how it operates.

Myth: "NFTs don't bring significance to the gaming industry" – This is yet another common misunderstanding about non-fungible tokens. There are a number of games out there that provide you the opportunity to gather NFTs. That indicates that these elements have the potential to raise the value of an NFT. After all, non-fungible tokens may be implemented in a wide variety of contexts, such as in the form of virtual objects in games like CryptoKitties and Spells of Genesis.

What Do I Stand To Earn If I Engage In Trading?

Some people are skeptical of cryptocurrencies like Bitcoin, while others see its potential to overtake traditional currencies as the most popular means of exchanging money for other goods and services. The fact that some businesses now accept Bitcoin as a form of payment demonstrates this argument. Users of Microsoft products, for example, have the option to pay for their purchases in the Windows and Xbox shops using bitcoin. Reddit, Overstock.com, and Expedia.com are among the online retailers that take bitcoin payments. Even Subway, which is famous for its fresh sandwiches, and Wikipedia, which is the biggest free encyclopedia available on the Internet, are getting on board with this trend.

The first item that you might get as a result of trading cryptocurrency is accessibility to this market. It is a known fact that the majority of people do not trust Bitcoin as a viable financial option. It is, nevertheless, on the increase, demonstrating a tenacious character in the face of a challenging financial market alongside precious metals and conventional fiat currencies. Moreover, it is competing well with conventional fiat currencies. The example that was provided in the preceding paragraph lends credence to the uncomplicated fact that the number of shops and businesses that are prepared to accept payments in a medium of exchange that is not based on fiat currency is growing.

Therefore, engaging in the trading of digital currencies may provide you with a head start that is helpful. If the current trajectory indicates that Bitcoin and other cryptocurrencies will become widely utilized in the not too distant future, then it is in your best interest to be one of the astute individuals who already has a few thousand dollars in his virtual pocket when something that was previously suspect becomes the usual.

Those individuals who have previously engaged in the practice of making conventional investments could find the next item that might be achieved from trading cryptocurrency to be more tempting. People's financial portfolios could benefit from the addition of cryptocurrencies, also known as alternative currencies since that's what some people choose to name them.

A "hedge" is a common phrase in the world of finance that refers to a technique that may protect a portfolio from experiencing a loss. This kind of approach is known as "hedging." Consider the example of individual X to better understand how hedging works. His investing portfolio contains somewhere around a hundred different shares of Company X. This company's primary source of revenue comes from the provision of remodeling services for commercial and residential properties. Now, when an economy is going through a recession, individuals will put their home improvement projects lower on their priority list. They would prioritize meeting their most fundamental need, such as ensuring that they have food to eat. Therefore, a person X would be hedging his portfolio if he also had some shares in Company Y, which is a dollar shop that focuses mostly on selling food products that are both inexpensive and simple to cook. Take note of how everything evens out.

Cryptocurrencies like Bitcoin have the potential to become your Company Y. They have the potential to be your savior in the event that an unforeseen circumstance causes the value of your other assets to plummet. However, you should avoid investing an excessive amount in your hedges. There is a reason why they are just contingency plans.

Trading digital currencies may provide you with those two primary benefits, which are the most important takeaways from the activity. Do you have any further ideas for possible benefits?

Starting To Invest

Now is the moment to make investments. Investing in cryptocurrencies is, for the most part, quite comparable to investing in any other kind of fund, which means that the fundamentals are same for both. To get to where you want to go, however, there are a lot of extra steps you need to do since crypto-investment is far more sophisticated than traditional investing.

Step one is to choose a coin and educate yourself about it. This phase is going to demand a significant amount of reading and thought. As was shown before, there is a diverse selection of coins available for investment, each of which is subject to its own unique trends and markets. Learn to evaluate, not simply admire, the industry you're putting yourself into by reading books, consulting specialists, and learning to analyze the market you're getting yourself into. Making sure that all of the material you are reading is as recent and up-to-date as possible is an essential component of this; reading statistics and studies from the past is not very helpful. The following are some characteristics of coins that might help you assess whether or not they are beneficial to you as a player:

The term "distribution of capital" refers to the proportion of the available funds that are held by various parties. The number of individuals who use a currency is the single most important factor in determining the risk that it will collapse. It is safer to invest in a coin that is extensively traded throughout the market by a large number of different individuals than it is to invest in a currency that is only dispersed among a small number of people.

What is the percentage of your money that is being returned to you? Is it the case that those who invest in it make a significant amount of money? When it comes to investing, the objective is to get a high Return on Investment (ROI). On a good day, investors investing in the top-selling coins are looking at returns on their investments worth millions of dollars, while others are seeing just hundreds. Keep in mind that the purpose of your visit is to generate money. Choose those that have a high turnover or return on investment.

The amount of time a coin has been available for purchase on the market is relevant to determining both its current value and its potential for future growth as an investment. If the currency in question has only been around for around two weeks, yet it has already made up into the Top 100 billboards, then there is a good chance that it is not particularly dependable or real. Even if there are situations in which this is due to a perfectly legitimate increase in one's financial standing, the majority of the time it is due to some form of fraudulent or criminal action. Examining the length of time a coin has been in circulation might serve as a good rule of thumb for determining its value. If it has been around for some time, has a high turnover rate, and has received positive evaluations, then there is a strong chance that it is a reputable source.

Alterations in the Value of the Coin: This refers to the rate at which the value of the coin is either rising or declining. When it comes to determining how well a coin is doing, the majority of the time, all you need to do is glance at a graphical depiction of its pricing. For instance, a rapid increase in value, followed by a quick decrease in value, is often indicative of either fraud or a problem on the company's end of things. It is strongly recommended that you do not put any money into purchasing that currency. Checking the amount of time it takes for a coin's price to reach its current level is one way to figure out whether or not it is a solid investment.

If you take a look at Bitcoin, you will see that its price rose extremely slowly until abruptly shooting up. This is a telltale indicator that the coin in question is probably trustworthy. Having said that, another thing you need to keep in mind is that it takes certain currencies some time before their prices go up. People won't invest in the beginning since there aren't any positive signals associated with the currency. However, as time goes on, they will ultimately cross a threshold and begin to see price and popularity increases as a result. Having the ability to anticipate when a coin will cross a certain barrier and buying it before it does so may be a highly profitable investment. A currency that is gaining in value entirely due to "hype" is something that you should make sure you keep an eye out for. These are the kinds of investments that are risky, unexpected, and only good for a very limited period of time.

The fashions were different when I wrote this book than they are now, when you are reading it, since the time has passed since I wrote it. This is more evidence that, in order to make an informed choice, you need to keep up to speed with the latest market trends on a daily basis. The following are some pointers that might assist you in staying current with current events and watching the progress of the market:

Influences on the Market Despite the fact that there are a lot of different reasons why the market might shift, it all boils down to one thing in the end, which is the requirement of the coin or money. If there is no purpose behind the currency, then it will not do very well in the market. In the same vein, if there is a significant demand for the coin, it will do rather well in the market. The performance of non-major coins may be better understood with the use of this information. It is important to keep in mind that larger coins such as Bitcoin will eventually catch up with the technology that these lesser-known cryptocurrencies use and overtake them. This may make investing in these lesser-known cryptocurrencies seem like a smart idea in the short term. Because of this, it is very necessary to maintain a watchful check not just on the market as a whole but also on the ins and outs of each new development.

Alterations in Technology: This is something that has a lot to do with the way in which the world is changing around the bitcoin industry. Because of the lightning-fast pace at which things are generated and developed in the digital age, there is the potential for a great number of unanticipated shifts to take place. Investigate any rapid shifts in technology that you become aware of, and determine whether or not these shifts are likely to have an effect on the cryptocurrency market.

Regarding their use in everyday life, how applicable do you find cryptocurrencies to be at the time of your investment? In what ways are they anticipated to be useful in the years to come? It's important to ask yourself these questions before making any investment, since the answers might determine the outcome of the transaction. One way to demonstrate your sense of realism is to consider the circumstances of other individuals. It could be worthwhile for someone to invest their money in the cryptocurrency market if they have a large amount of money lying around that they don't know what to do with. If you don't need a genuine currency for anything, why not attempt to make some money off of it?

When it comes to investing, confidence is one of the most important factors to consider, and no, this has nothing to do with how confident you are in your own investment (remember, you should never invest based on emotion). This is related to the level of faith that the general public has in the market as a whole. The fact that the market is not regulated makes it exceptionally susceptible to changes in the environment. Less meddling from governments or more "hype" around a particular coin are examples of factors that might lead to increased levels of trust. In circumstances like these, the cost of the currency is likely to go through the roof. On the other hand, there are a number of possibilities that might lead to a decline. People may have a loss of faith in the market as a result of factors such as severe government regulation or waves of hacking. As a direct consequence of this, the price of the currency will plummet to an all-time low. If you have the ability to forecast these changes, it will be easier for you to choose whether or not to invest your money in that particular currency.

Get Rid of Popularity: If the value of a coin suddenly shoots up, you should investigate the reason why. If the success of the currency can be attributed to nothing more than "hype" or popularity, it is probably best to avoid investing in it. This is due to the fact that, in the vast majority of cases, these increases do not last for an extended period of time and will result in a bad investment with significant losses.

In order for a system to be regarded as a cryptocurrency, it is essential that unequivocal evidence of ownership of the monetary units be provided. This entails using a cryptographic hash to encrypt the transaction data that is being stored on the blockchain. The use of cryptography to prevent tampering with the data after it has been timestamped helps to guarantee that transaction records are not altered in any way. As a result of this safeguarding of the transaction data, every single unit of bitcoin can be accounted for at each and every address to which it is transmitted and received. The private keys that are used to access the cryptocurrency held in digital wallets are safely and securely maintained on the blockchain. These wallets are accessible only by their owners. For instance, the creation of each Bitcoin is tracked and verified by recording and encrypting the transfer of each and every unit that is produced, sent, and received.

To have a grasp on the various range of cryptocurrencies now available, we must first get familiar with the coin that started it all. Bitcoin is the name of the first cryptocurrency ever created. Additionally, it is the kind of cryptocurrency that has the most users. Bitcoin, like the blockchain technology it is founded on, may be thought of as a symbol for gold. It is extracted in the same manner as a natural resource, and with time an increasing amount of processing power is needed to extract it. Similar to gold, it does have certain useful applications, but its primary function is that of a money that can be exchanged for other products and services. It is not extracted from the ground in the same way that gold is. The computation of cryptographic arithmetic on computers is required for the mining process of cryptocurrencies; however, this topic will be discussed further on.

What determines the value of a cryptocurrency? Cryptocurrencies are often denoted by their underlying units of currency, which are referred to as cryptocoins. There is no set standard for how much one cryptocoin is worth when converted to fiat cash. The value of a cryptocoin is determined by the number of individuals who trade with it and are willing to accept it as payment for products and services. When Bitcoin was originally introduced, its value in US dollars ranged from almost nothing to a tiny fraction of a penny. This was because Bitcoin was still in its infancy at the time. The value of one bitcoin rose in tandem with the cryptocurrency's rising profile among users. To the same extent as any other form of money, the value of a cryptocurrency is determined by what other people are willing to pay for it.

Blockchain technology has to be comprehended first before we can have any hope of comprehending cryptocurrencies at its most fundamental level. Even though we will go into further detail on blockchain in the upcoming chapter, having a fundamental knowledge of it is necessary in order to grasp the fundamentals of cryptocurrencies. In order to do this, we are going to describe the structure of the blockchain using more abstract language. To begin, there are the individual blocks that comprise a cryptocurrency network. The "chains" that connect each of these individual blocks are the next topic. While more specific information develop a more in-depth grasp, having a fundamental understanding of how the underlying structure operates provides a functioning notion of what is being discussed. After we finish going through the fundamentals, we will spend some time developing this workable notion.

One kind of data structure is referred to as a "block" in a blockchain. The structure of a cryptocurrency is built from the information that is stored in the blocks, which may be of a range of different sorts. This data consists of network transaction information, a cryptographic hash of the previous block, a timestamp that cannot be altered, information that identifies the user, the complexity of the hashing process, and more. These blocks are accessible to every participant in a blockchain, and they include all of the data required to maintain a record of who has which cryptocurrencies and where they are moving those cryptocurrencies. These chunks of information are entirely secure against any kind of alteration or hacking because to the use of cryptography, which will be discussed in further detail later on in this chapter.

The "chain" that connects all of the blocks in a blockchain is really embedded into each block itself. This makes the blockchain very secure. As was indicated before, the contents of each block include a cryptographic hash of the block that came before it. This is the information from the previous block that has been encrypted into an unbreakable secret code and saved in the block that is now being processed. This is the element that holds the blocks in place. The very first block is the only one that does not include a cryptographic hash of the previous blocks; all other blocks do. Because of this, the very first block is also often referred to as the "genesis block." It is possible to follow every block on the blockchain, including forks and other variations, all the way back to the original genesis block.

By combining these two components, we can begin to get a fundamental understanding of what the blockchain really is. We have a functional grasp of how bitcoin operates, provided that we have a fundamental idea of what the blockchain is. Blocks are recordings of transaction information that include essential identifying data inside their own bodies. Blocks are the building blocks of cryptocurrencies. An encrypted hash of the contents from the previous block is one example of such a piece of data. The chain is created when encrypted hashes are used to link one block to the one that came before it. As a group, we now have a blockchain, which may be defined as a chain of transaction records that are both protected and encrypted using cryptography. With the use of these transaction records, we are able to get a comprehensive understanding of who is in possession of which cryptocurrencies and where they are being transported.

www.ingramcontent.com/pod-product-compliance
Lightning Source LLC
Chambersburg PA
CBHW071226210326
41597CB00016B/1959